BUILDING BRIDGES

Lessons from a Pittsburgh Partnership to Strengthen
Systems of Care for Maternal Depression

Executive Summary

Donna J. Keyser | Ellen Burke Beckjord | Ray Firth

Sarah Frith | Susan L. Lovejoy | Sajith Pillai

Dana Schultz | Harold Alan Pincus

Sponsored by UPMC *for You*

RAND HEALTH

This work was conducted under contract with UPMC *for You*. It was funded by a consortium of local and state organizations. The research was performed in RAND Health, a division of the RAND Corporation.

Library of Congress Cataloging-in-Publication Data is available for this publication.

ISBN 978-0-8330-5009-0

The RAND Corporation is a nonprofit research organization providing objective analysis and effective solutions that address the challenges facing the public and private sectors around the world. RAND's publications do not necessarily reflect the opinions of its research clients and sponsors.

RAND® is a registered trademark.

Cover design by Pete Soriano

Published 2010 by the RAND Corporation
1776 Main Street, P.O. Box 2138, Santa Monica, CA 90407-2138
1200 South Hayes Street, Arlington, VA 22202-5050
4570 Fifth Avenue, Suite 600, Pittsburgh, PA 15213-2665
RAND URL: http://www.rand.org/
To order RAND documents or to obtain additional information, contact
Distribution Services: Telephone: (310) 451-7002;
Fax: (310) 451-6915; Email: order@rand.org

Preface

This summary offers a synopsis of a complete report[1] of the Allegheny County Maternal Depression Initiative, conducted by the Allegheny County Maternal and Child Health Care Collaborative between January 1, 2007, and June 30, 2010. The RAND–University of Pittsburgh Health Institute (RUPHI) convened the collaborative in January 2002 with support from The Heinz Endowments. Its mission is to build a model system of care for mothers and young children in Allegheny County, Pennsylvania. The Allegheny County Maternal Depression Initiative represents the third phase of the collaborative's work. The initiative was supported by a consortium of local funders and the Pennsylvania Department of Public Welfare.

With leadership from the University of Pittsburgh Medical Center (UPMC) Health Plan and the Allegheny County Department of Human Services, Office of Behavioral Health, initiative partners sought to improve the capacity of local systems of care for identifying women at high risk for maternal depression, enhancing their access to available resources and services, and engaging them in behavioral health treatment as needed and appropriate. The RUPHI project team, under contract with UPMC *for You*, was responsible for working with collaborative members to design, implement, and evaluate the initiative. The recommendations were developed by the RUPHI team with input from a subset of collaborative leaders and initiative partners.

The information presented in the report should prove useful to a wide range of stakeholders interested in mobilizing their communities to improve health care service delivery and outcomes, especially among traditionally underserved populations. The results and lessons learned will be especially relevant for communities in which maternal depression has been identified as a high-priority public health issue. Although the work of the collaborative was focused on improving practice and policy related to maternal depression within the Medicaid system in Allegheny County and, by extension, the broader Pennsylvania Medicaid managed care system, the overall approach could be extended to other populations and communities in the commonwealth and beyond.

---

[1] Keyser DJ, Beckjord EB, Firth R, Frith S, Lovejoy SL, Pillai S, et al. *Building Bridges: Lessons from a Pittsburgh Partnership to Strengthen Systems of Care for Maternal Depression*. Santa Monica, CA: RAND Corporation, 2010.

Questions and comments about this summary are welcome and should be addressed to the RUPHI project director:

Donna J. Keyser, PhD, MBA
Management Scientist
RAND Corporation
4570 Fifth Avenue, Suite 600
Pittsburgh, PA 15213
Tel: (412) 683-2300 x4928
Fax: (412) 683-2800
Donna_Keyser@rand.org

Contents

Figures

Tables

Acknowledgments

The RUPHI project team, on behalf of the Allegheny County Maternal and Child Health Care Collaborative, extends its sincerest gratitude to UPMC Health Plan and the Allegheny County Department of Human Services, Office of Behavioral Health. Without the leadership and support of these two organizations, the work of the initiative would not have been possible. In particular, we owe a very special thanks to the visionary leaders of the initiative, John Lovelace, president, UPMC *for You*, and chief program officer, Community Care, and Patricia L. Valentine, deputy director, Allegheny County Department of Human Services, Office of Behavioral Health.

We further acknowledge with gratitude the many individuals and organizations that participated in the Allegheny County Maternal Depression Initiative, and the local and state funders that supported our work. These organizations, and the leadership teams within them, are listed in the appendix. We recognize and thank our funders in particular. These include UPMC Health Plan, Highmark Foundation, Staunton Farm Foundation, FISA Foundation, the Eden Hall Foundation, and the Pennsylvania Department of Public Welfare.

For their important contributions to the report, we thank Kristin Leuschner and Kathryn Giglio, communications analysts from RAND, and peer reviewers Helen Cahalane of the University of Pittsburgh and Melony Sorbero of RAND.

Finally, and perhaps most importantly, we thank all of the unnamed families in Allegheny County who have worked with the collaborative over the years to build a model system of care that will better serve mothers and young children in our community.

Abbreviations

EPDS   Edinburgh Postnatal Depression Scale

MCO   managed care organization

ONAF   obstetrical needs assessment form

PHQ-2   Patient Health Questionnaire 2

RUPHI   RAND–University of Pittsburgh Health Institute

UPMC   University of Pittsburgh Medical Center

Executive Summary

Maternal depression is a widespread public health issue that takes a toll on the well-being and livelihood of mothers and their families. It demands a strong community response involving people who share a common vision to strengthen the health and resilience of all mothers and their families in need of help and support.[1]

Between January 2007 and June 2010, members of the Allegheny County Maternal and Child Health Care Collaborative—a broad-based community coalition that has been operating in Allegheny County, Pennsylvania, since 2002—designed, implemented, and evaluated the Allegheny County Maternal Depression Initiative. The initiative is a local systems-change effort focused on increasing identification, referrals, and engagement in treatment as needed and appropriate for women at high risk for maternal depression. This summary describes how and why the initiative was created, the processes through which it was implemented and evaluated, and the results and lessons learned. It concludes with recommendations for practice and policy change designed to expand and sustain the initiative's achievements.

The Problem

Documented high rates of prevalence, especially among low-income populations, combined with significant adverse consequences for both mother and child, make maternal depression the number one complication of childbirth in the United States. Empirical research has demonstrated that interventions for depression are effective for both the general population and ethnically diverse and impoverished groups.[2] Nevertheless, for

---

[1] Mental Health America and National Center for Children in Poverty. *Maternal Depression: Making a Difference Through Community Action: A Planning Guide*. Alexandria, VA: Mental Health America; 2008.

[2] Miranda J, Chung JY, Green BL, et al. Treating depression in predominantly low-income young minority women: a randomized controlled trial. *JAMA*. 2003;290(1):57-65.

many reasons, women with maternal depression are not identified, and, even when they are identified, they are not effectively engaged in treatment.[3]

Barriers to identifying and treating women with maternal depression exist in numerous forms and on many different levels, as documented in the literature and through the collaborative's work, including the following:

- Many physicians do not routinely screen for maternal depression using a validated instrument.
- Capacity for appropriately triaging, referring, and treating women at high risk for maternal depression is limited in many physical health care settings.
- Existing gaps between the physical and behavioral health care systems make care coordination difficult.
- Consumer access is impeded by cultural, perceptual, and real-life issues and stressors that are not easily resolved.
- Available treatment protocols might not meet the needs and preferences of pregnant or postpartum women.

Aims and Focus of the Initiative

Since low-income women are at higher risk for maternal depression than other women[4] and less likely to receive adequate care,[5] the collaborative chose to focus its systems-change efforts on improving service delivery for maternal depression within the local Medicaid system. The initiative had three aims:

---

[3] Swartz HA, Shear MK, Wren FJ, et al. Depression and anxiety among mothers who bring their children to a pediatric mental health clinic. *Psychiatr Serv.* 2005;56:1077-1083.

[4] Lanzi RG, Pascoe JM, Keltner B, Ramey SL. Correlates of maternal depressive symptoms in a national Head Start program sample. *Arch Pediatr Adolesc Med.* 1999;153(8):801-807; Miranda J, Green BL. The need for mental health services research focusing on poor young women. *J Ment Health Policy Econ.* 1999;2(2):73-80; Onunaku N. *Improving Maternal and Infant Mental Health: Focus on Maternal Depression.* Los Angeles, CA: National Center for Infant and Early Childhood Health Policy; 2005; Siefert K, Bowman PJ, Heflin CM, Danziger S, Williams DR. Social and environmental predictors of maternal depression in current and recent welfare recipients. *Am J Orthopsychiatry.* 2000;70(4):510-522.

[5] Agency for Healthcare Research and Quality. *National Healthcare Disparities Report: Summary.* Rockville, MD: Agency for Healthcare Research and Quality, 2004; Skaer TL, Sclar DA, Robison LM, Galin RS. Trends in the rate of depressive illness and use of antidepressant pharmacotherapy by ethnicity/race: an assessment of office-based visits in the United States, 1992–1997. *Clin Ther.* 2000;22(12):1575-1589; Wang PS, Berglund P, Kessler RC. Recent care of common mental disorders in the United States: prevalence and conformance with evidence-based recommendations. *J Gen Intern Med.* 2000;15(5):284-292; Young AS, Klap R, Sherbourne CD, Wells KB. The quality of care for depressive and anxiety disorders in the United States. *Arch Gen Psychiatry.* 2001;58(1):55-61; Vesga-López O, Blanco C, Keyes K, Olfson M, Grant BF, Hasin DS. Psychiatric disorders in pregnant and postpartum women in the United States. *Arch Gen Psychiatry.* 2008;65(7):805-815.

- to improve the identification of maternal depression among Medicaid-eligible pregnant and postpartum women in Allegheny County
- to enhance access to available resources and services for women who screen positive for maternal depression
- to increase engagement in behavioral health treatment as needed and appropriate.

To this end, three components of service delivery were targeted for improvement at the systems level: screening, referral, and engagement in treatment.

The Conceptual Model of Systems Change

Figure S.1 presents the initiative's conceptual model of systems change.[6] This model recognizes that consumers and families are at the center of the process, signifying the intent of the local Medicaid managed care system to create a "safety net" around women at high risk for maternal depression. It further acknowledges the roles of key stakeholder groups in driving and sustaining practice and policy improvements. Strengthening linkages between these groups is essential for achieving the initiative's aims and, in so doing, ensuring that the system better meets the needs and preferences of women at high risk for maternal depression.

Operational Framework of the Initiative

The collaborative developed a protocol for the initiative that delineated the roles and responsibilities of key stakeholder groups in accordance with best-practice standards, the capacities and stated preferences of individual participating practices, and network provider requirements as set forth in the state contract for Medicaid managed care services. Table S.1 provides a brief description of these roles and responsibilities for key partners in each stakeholder group.

The protocol was implemented in two phases:

---

6   Adapted from Pincus HA, Pechura CM, Elinson L, Pettit AR. Depression in primary care: linking clinical and systems strategies. *Gen Hosp Psychiatry*. 2001;23(6):311-318; Pincus HA. The future of behavioral health and primary care: drowning in the mainstream or left on the bank? *Psychosomatics*. 2003;44(1):1-11; Pincus HA, Hough L, Houtsinger JK, Rollman BL, Frank RG. Emerging models of depression care: multi-level ('6 P') strategies. *Int J Methods Psychiatr Res*. 2003;12(1):54-63; Pincus HA, Houtsinger JK, Bachman J, Keyser D. Depression in primary care: bringing behavioral health care into the mainstream. *Health Aff*. 2005;4(1):271-276; Pincus HA, Pechura C, Keyser D, Bachman J, Houtsinger JK. Depression in primary care: learning lessons in a national quality improvement program. *Adm Policy Ment Health Ment Health Serv Res*. 2006;33(1, theme issue):2-15.

Figure S.1
Conceptual Model of Systems Change

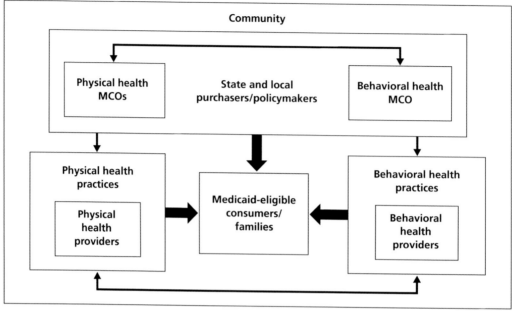

RAND *MG973-S.1*

- Phase 1 implementation (December 2007–December 2008) focused on implementing and tracking the screening and referral components of the initiative protocol.
- Phase 2 implementation (January 2009–February 2010) incorporated efforts to design and test various strategies for increasing referrals of women who screened positive for maternal depression to local physical health managed care organization (MCO) care managers for needed supports and services and enhancing their engagement in behavioral health treatment as needed and appropriate.

Over the course of the initiative, the collaborative also designed and carried out a range of strategies to support the implementation of the protocol and to ensure the overall success of the systems-change process. These strategies, which involved all stakeholder groups, are summarized in Table S.2 by phase of implementation. Based on the results of the phase 1 implementation, the collaborative modified and added components during phase 2.

Initiative Evaluation Plan

The collaborative designed a mixed-methods approach, using both qualitative and quantitative data, to evaluate the initiative. The evaluation indicators and data-

Table S.1
Initiative Partners and Their Roles and Responsibilities, by Key Stakeholder Group

Stakeholder Group	Description	Roles and Responsibilities
Medicaid-eligible consumers and families	Pregnant women or mothers with children under age 1 in Allegheny County presenting for care at a physical health practice participating in the initiative	The initiative's target population and critical source of information on the needs and preferences of Medicaid-eligible women in Allegheny County
Physical health practices and providers in the HealthChoices network[a]	10 pediatrics, obstetrics and gynecology, and family medicine sites and their affiliated providers	Systematically screen target population for maternal depression using a validated screening tool; enhance access to available supports and services via referral; support the initiative's data-collection efforts
HealthChoices physical health MCOs	UPMC *for You*, Gateway Health Plan, Unison Health Plan, and their affiliated leaders and care management staff	Respond to referrals for members who screened positive for maternal depression; connect to behavioral health services as appropriate; serve as the system's "safety net" for the target population; support the initiative's data-collection efforts
Behavioral health practices and providers in the HealthChoices network	A range of practices offering behavioral health treatment for maternal depression and their affiliated providers	Provide evidence-based treatments that meet consumers' needs and preferences
HealthChoices behavioral health MCO	Community Care and its affiliated leaders and care management staff	Work with initiative partners to arrange behavioral health treatment as needed and appropriate; support the initiative's data-collection efforts
State and local purchasers and policymakers	Pennsylvania Department of Public Welfare, Allegheny County Department of Human Services, Pennsylvania Department of Health; Allegheny County Health Department; and their affiliated leaders and staff	Establish guidelines and standards, performance measures, review processes, and related strategies for ensuring that state contractual requirements are appropriate for meeting the needs of pregnant and postpartum women served through the HealthChoices program; support related data-collection efforts as needed
Other organizations in the community	Local funders, RUPHI, home-based service providers	Offer peripheral supports to ensure sustainable systems change

NOTE: Community Care = Community Care Behavioral Health Organization.

[a] HealthChoices manages Medical Assistance (Medicaid) in Allegheny County.

Table S.2
Summary of Strategies to Support Protocol Implementation During Phases 1 and 2

Targeted Area of Focus	Phase 1 Strategy	Phase 2 Strategy
Education and training of consumers and providers	Educational pamphlet about maternal depression and list of community resources Provider training programs on use of validated maternal depression screening tool, referral, and engagement Website	Additional consumer-supportive materials (e.g., "Prescription for Good Health") Provider training sessions on mood disorders and motivational interviewing skills[a] Policy forum on maternal depression practice and policy Educational and networking workshop on home-based service programs Public forum to disseminate initiative findings and recommendations
Listening and responding to consumers' needs	Consumer focus groups Participation in prenatal support groups	Focus on home-based service options
Use of evidence-based tools and protocols for depression screening and triage	EPDS with varying high-risk thresholds across practices, PHQ-2, and psychiatric history Decision tool for triaging consumers who screened positive	
Pathways and related infrastructure to support integrated care	Common referral fax form Procedures for obtaining informed consent All-partners meetings	Use of warm transfers Efforts to improve communication between physical health providers and MCO care managers and consumers
Performance measurement and shared data collection to assess progress and inform ongoing improvement	Agreed-upon performance measures and data-collection procedures Ongoing analysis and information sharing Course corrections as needed	Stakeholder group discussions

NOTE: EPDS = Edinburgh Postnatal Depression Scale. PHQ-2 = Patient Health Questionnaire 2.

[a] Motivational interviewing is a brief, person-centered, goal-oriented counseling method for enhancing a person's self-motivation for change by working with and resolving ambivalence.

collection instruments and data sources can be organized into two broad categories: organizational indicators and data-collection instruments and clinical indicators and data sources. The organizational indicators captured key features of systems change related to consumer and provider attitudes and behaviors; the clinical indicators captured key features of systems change related to care processes aligned with the initiative's three aims. Figure S.2 illustrates how the data-collection tools and data sources align with the progression of a pregnant or postpartum woman through the processes of screening, referral, and engagement in treatment.

Figure S.2
Alignment of Data-Collection Tools and Data Sources with the Progression of a Pregnant or Postpartum Woman Through the Screening, Referral, and Engagement Processes

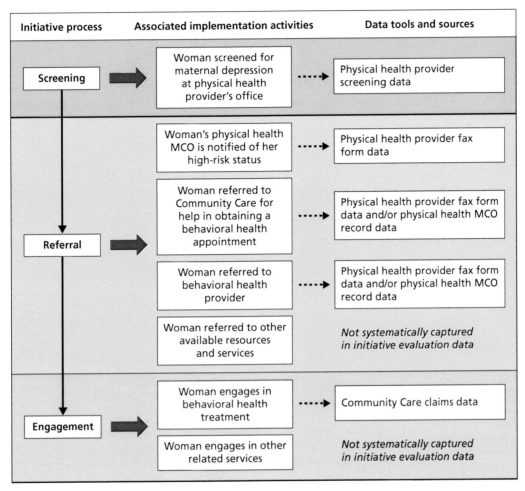

Results of the Initiative

Although it is not possible to disentangle specific cause-effect relationships among the strategies that were implemented as part of the initiative and the outcomes that were achieved, the results clearly show that, taken as a whole, the collaborative was successful in improving key organizational and clinical processes related to the achievement of its three aims, particularly as compared to reference points cited in the literature related to maternal depression screening, referral, and engagement in treatment for pregnant and postpartum women (Figure S.3).

Aim 1: To improve the identification of maternal depression among Medicaid-eligible pregnant and postpartum women in Allegheny County. Between December 2007 and December 2009, physical health providers participating in the initiative completed more than 8,500 screens on pregnant and postpartum women. Although the overall screening rate declined somewhat from phase 1 to phase 2, the overall 54-percent screening rate across all practices represents a significant accomplishment. The vast majority (86 percent) of participating physical health providers reported that they often, almost always, or always screened for maternal depression at a woman's first prenatal care or postpartum visit using a validated screening tool. Nonetheless, increasing the screening rate represents a clear target for continued quality improvement.

Figure S.3
Summary of Initiative Results

	Reference point	Phase 1 results	Phase 2 results	Overall results
Screening				
Estimated total number of visits at participating physical health practices	NA	6,419	9,272	15,692
Screening rate (%)	4–25	59	52	54
Percentage of positive screens	13–25	24 (n = 3,758)	26 (n = 4,789)	25 (n = 8,547)
Referral				
Referral rate among those who screen positive (%)	50	47 (n = 234)	65 (n = 431)	57 (n = 665)
Engagement				
Percentage of referred women contacted by physical health MCO care manager	NA	65	43	53
Engagement rate among those referred (%)	20	51 (n = 72)	44 (n = 113)	46 (n = 195)
Percentage of engaged women who have at least 3 behavioral health claims	NA	60	57	60

NOTE: NA = not available.
RAND *MG973-S.3*

Aim 2: To enhance access to available resources and services for women who screen positive for maternal depression. Among the nearly 1,200 women identified as high risk by a positive screen, 57 percent were referred by the provider to their physical health MCO care managers. Overall, the referral rate improved from 47 percent in phase 1 to 65 percent in phase 2. Participating physical health providers also reported an increase in the frequency with which they referred women who screened positive to physical health MCO care managers. Overall, MCO care managers were able to reach just over half (53 percent) of their high-risk members. Improving this rate of contact and decreasing the average time between referral and first contact remain critical goals for the physical health MCO care managers.

Aim 3: To increase engagement in behavioral health treatment as needed and appropriate. Nearly one-half (46 percent) of the high-risk women referred had engaged in behavioral health treatment at some point. While some of these women engaged in behavioral health treatment prior to the referral, 35 percent of referred women engaged in behavioral health treatment after being identified as being at high risk for maternal depression, which is considerably higher than the 20-percent engagement rate recently published for a similar population.[7] However, more work should be done to increase initial and sustained engagement in behavioral health treatment.

In other areas, the collaborative confronted challenges. For example, over the course of the initiative, it was difficult to ensure consistent and timely communication among those with shared responsibility for high-risk women. While the initiative protocol sought to open communication channels, in practice, the information did not always reach the individuals who needed it. Further, there was a considerable lag between a woman's identification and referral and her ultimate engagement in behavioral health treatment, representing a target for continued quality improvement over time.

Top Ten Lessons Learned

In order to identify and prioritize the most important lessons learned through this initiative, the RUPHI team compared the results of the stakeholder group discussions held at the end of the initiative with quantitative and qualitative results that were collected over the course of the initiative. The resulting ten lessons listed here are described in more detail in the full report.

1. There is no such thing as too much education or training on issues related to maternal depression, but training is not enough.

---

[7]   Miranda J, Chung JY, Green BL, et al. Treating depression in predominantly low-income young minority women: a randomized controlled trial. *JAMA.* 2003;290(1):57-65.

2. Numerous factors influence the needs and preferences of women who are at high risk for maternal depression.
3. Families' negative views of or disappointing previous experiences with mental health services or referrals are pervasive and strong.
4. Physical health practices can integrate routine screening for maternal depression into the clinical care process.
5. Referrals within and across systems are difficult to execute.
6. The more links in the chain from screening to referral to engagement in treatment, the more likely the chain is to break, but shortening the chain is not a guaranteed solution.
7. Co-location can work if co-located providers are truly integrated into the care team.
8. Diffusion of responsibility in complex systems might not be completely avoidable, but it is remediable.
9. Effective health care requires transparency and sharing of information among providers and patients.
10. Clear expectations, performance measurement, agreed-upon quality standards, and mechanisms for accountability are key drivers of systems improvement.

Recommendations for Policy and Practice Change

Given the long-term, significant impact that maternal depression can have on maternal, child, and family health, the priority the state has placed on bridging existing gaps between physical and behavioral health care in the Medicaid system, and the obvious need for continued improvement related to maternal depression screening, referral, and engagement in treatment, the RUPHI team offers four sets of practice and policy recommendations for key stakeholder groups. These recommendations are provided in detail in Tables S.3–S.6.

Next Steps for the Collaborative

The collaborative has recently embarked on an expansion of the Allegheny County Maternal Depression Initiative, which serves as one concrete next step toward systems integration and holistic interventions for parents and children. The collaborative's new initiative—Helping Families Raise Healthy Children—advances the work of the collaborative in three ways. First, it builds important linkages with an additional sector that provides services to families with children ages 0 to 3 in Allegheny County—namely, the early-intervention system. Second, it expands maternal depression screening to all primary caregivers with young children who enter the early-intervention system

Table S.3
Recommendations to Improve Identification of Maternal Depression

Stakeholder	Recommendation
Pennsylvania General Assembly	Universal screening is the first step in a comprehensive state strategy designed to ensure that more women with maternal depression receive services as needed and appropriate. However, nothing more than additional screening will be accomplished without adequate capacity and explicit processes for referring women who screen positive for maternal depression to an array of accessible, effective, and culturally informed services that meet their needs and preferences. In this context, we recommend the following: A. Mandate universal screening for maternal depression irrespective of insurance coverage. B. Legislation mandating universal screening should also ensure that (1) the Department of Public Welfare and the Department of Insurance[a] develop adequate capacity for timely referrals and treatment of publicly and privately insured pregnant and postpartum women who screen positive for maternal depression and (2) the Department of Public Welfare and the Department of Insurance, along with the Department of Health, are involved in adopting and promulgating rules and regulations necessary to carry out the purposes and provisions of this legislation.
HealthChoices physical health MCOs	A. Establish maternal depression screening requirements for network providers who serve pregnant and postpartum women. These requirements should be consistent with evidence-based screening practices and professional organization standards and specify (1) validated screening tools acceptable for use, (2) appropriate screening intervals, (3) a common threshold for identifying probable maternal depression. B. Revise existing perinatal depression measures or create new measures that align with evidence-based practices and standards for maternal depression screening. C. Set explicit targets for improving the rate of maternal depression screening across network providers who serve pregnant and postpartum women. D. Establish reporting, monitoring, and feedback systems to assess and improve the maternal depression screening performance of network providers. E. Develop, implement, and evaluate various strategies to support network providers in meeting and exceeding their performance goals.
Physical health practices and providers in the HealthChoices network	A. Accelerate efforts to screen all pregnant and postpartum women with an acceptable validated screening tool, at the appropriate intervals, and using a common threshold for identifying probable maternal depression. B. To the extent possible, incorporate an acceptable, validated maternal depression screening tool into the practice's electronic medical record.

[a] The Pennsylvania Department of Insurance is responsible for administering the laws of the commonwealth as they pertain to the regulation of the insurance industry, in order to protect the insurance consumer.

Table S.4
Recommendations to Enhance Access to Available Resources and Services for Women Who Screen Positive for Maternal Depression

Stakeholder	Recommendation
Pennsylvania Department of Public Welfare, Office of Medical Assistance Programs and Office of Mental Health and Substance Abuse Services	The HealthChoices agreement has extensive requirements for written agreements and protocols related to access and coordination among physical and behavioral health MCOs and providers. These requirements are intended to maximize outreach efforts to members identified as needing services and to facilitate referrals and continuity of care as needed. The Department of Public Welfare regularly reviews these agreements and protocols. However, significant challenges remain with regard to ensuring successful outreach to members with maternal depression and their subsequent access to needed services. In this context, we recommend the following: A. Review and revise the current requirements in order to ensure their appropriateness for meeting the outreach and access needs of pregnant and postpartum members who screen positive for maternal depression. B. More explicitly delineate the roles and responsibilities of MCOs and network providers for implementing the revised requirements. C. Strengthen the current review process by establishing performance measures to properly assess the extent to which contractual requirements lead to (1) successful outreach to pregnant and postpartum members who screen positive for maternal depression and (2) improved service access as needed by these members. D. Develop, implement, and evaluate various strategies to support MCOs in meeting the contractual requirements.
HealthChoices physical and behavioral health MCOs	A. Establish explicit collaborative procedures involving MCO care management staff and network providers for making, receiving, and handling referrals of pregnant and postpartum members who screen positive for maternal depression. These procedures should include (1) an appropriately safeguarded electronic means for sharing necessary patient information among all relevant parties; (2) effective strategies for connecting with members, assessing their needs and health status, and responding appropriately; and (3) provision of timely feedback to referring providers on patient status and relevant outcomes. B. Revise existing perinatal depression measures or create new measures that align with the established referral procedures. C. Set explicit targets for increasing referrals of pregnant and postpartum members who screen positive for maternal depression to MCO care managers or behavioral health or other service providers as appropriate, and improving the process through which these referrals are handled. D. Establish reporting, monitoring, and feedback systems to assess and improve the referral performance of network providers and MCO care management staff. Incorporate measures of provider, MCO care management, and member satisfaction in the ongoing review process. E. Develop, implement, and evaluate various strategies to support network providers and MCO care management staff in meeting and exceeding their performance goals. F. Review member incentive and reward programs for opportunities to further encourage pregnant and postpartum women who screen positive for maternal depression to connect with their MCO care managers on a regular basis.
HealthChoices physical health MCOs	Revise the ONAF to include the EPDS or other acceptable depression screening score for all pregnant women.

Table S.4—Continued

Stakeholder	Recommendation
HealthChoices behavioral health MCOs	Evaluate the benefits of placing a behavioral health care manager in large-volume physical health practices. Develop a detailed plan for (1) integrating the individual or function into the practice's work flow and providing access to relevant information systems; (2) fully utilizing motivational interview techniques and patient-centered principles, with a strong focus on addressing the member's tangible social support needs (e.g., transportation, childcare); (3) assessing patient and family outcomes for engagement in behavioral health services or appropriate alternatives. To enable physical health providers to become sufficiently familiar with the access requirements and range of services and providers available through the behavioral health network, allow the co-location strategy to achieve its maximum level of implementation (at least one year) before making a final assessment of its value and sustainability.
Physical health practices and providers in the HealthChoices network	Accelerate efforts to refer pregnant and postpartum women who screen positive for maternal depression to physical and behavioral health MCOs, behavioral health providers, or community resources and services (e.g., home-based service programs) as needed and appropriate.

NOTE: ONAF = obstetrical needs assessment form.

Table S.5
Recommendations to Increase Engagement in Behavioral Health Treatment as Needed and Appropriate

Stakeholder	Recommendation
Pennsylvania Department of Public Welfare, Office of Medical Assistance Programs and Office of Mental Health and Substance Abuse Services	The HealthChoices Agreement has extensive requirements for written agreements and protocols related to access and coordination among physical and behavioral health MCOs and providers. These requirements are intended to facilitate members' access to diagnostic assessment and treatment, prescribing practices, and other treatment issues necessary for optimal health. The Department of Public Welfare regularly reviews these agreements and protocols. However, significant challenges remain with regard to engaging members with maternal depression in behavioral health treatment as needed and appropriate. In this context, we recommend the following: A. Review and revise the current requirements in order to ensure their appropriateness for meeting the treatment engagement needs of pregnant and postpartum women who screen positive for maternal depression. B. More explicitly delineate the roles and responsibilities of MCOs and network providers for implementing the revised requirements. C. Strengthen the current review process by establishing performance measures to properly assess the extent to which the contractual requirements lead to engagement of members with maternal depression in behavioral health treatment. D. Develop, implement, and evaluate various strategies to support MCOs in meeting the contractual requirements.
HealthChoices physical and behavioral health MCOs	A. Establish explicit collaborative procedures involving MCO care management staff and network providers for facilitating engagement in behavioral health treatment among pregnant and postpartum members who screen positive for maternal depression. These procedures should include (1) an appropriately safeguarded electronic means for sharing necessary patient information among all relevant parties; (2) effective strategies for connecting with members, assessing their needs and health status, and responding appropriately; and (3) provision of timely feedback to referring providers on patient status and relevant outcomes. B. Revise existing perinatal depression measures or create new measures that align with the established engagement procedures. C. Set explicit targets for increasing engagement in behavioral health treatment for pregnant and postpartum members who screen positive for maternal depression. D. Establish reporting, monitoring, and feedback systems to assess and improve the performance of network providers and MCO care management staff specific to engaging members who screen positive for maternal depression in behavioral health care. Incorporate measures of provider, MCO care management, and member satisfaction in the ongoing review process. E. Develop, implement, and evaluate various strategies to support network providers and MCO care management staff in meeting and exceeding their performance goals. F. Review member incentive and reward programs for opportunities to further encourage pregnant and postpartum women who screen positive for maternal depression to engage in behavioral health treatment as needed and appropriate. G. In cases in which pregnant or postpartum women who screen positive for maternal depression will not accept a referral for outpatient mental health treatment, utilize and assess the cost-effectiveness of engaging them in home-based service programs or other nonmedical community programs.

Table S.5—Continued

Stakeholder	Recommendation
HealthChoices behavioral health MCOs	The combined negative impact of the attributions of illness, difficult life circumstances (e.g., poverty), demands of infant caretaking, and unfavorable perceptions or past experiences with the behavioral health system too often impedes access to treatment for women with maternal depression. Overcoming these barriers would lead to maternal recovery and healthy early child development. In this context, it is critical to ensure adequate, sufficiently skilled psychiatric capacity to meet HealthChoices' access standards and the treatment needs of pregnant and postpartum members with depression. Strategies to consider include the following: A. As rates of maternal depression screening increase, retest the utility and cost-effectiveness of a statewide telephone consultation service operated by psychiatrists to support providers (e.g., family medicine and other primary care practitioners) on issues related to diagnoses, treatment options, medications, or alternative therapies for pregnant and postpartum members who screen positive for maternal depression. B. Test the effectiveness and long-term viability of telephone or in-home mobile psychotherapy for pregnant and postpartum members who screen positive for maternal depression, as well as more innovative approaches, such as offering web-based cognitive behavioral therapy in multiple, family-friendly settings. C. Evaluate the benefits of placing a behavioral health specialist in large-volume physical health practices. Develop a detailed plan for (1) integrating the individual or function into the practice's clinical work flow and providing access to relevant information systems; (2) fully utilizing motivational interview techniques and patient-centered principles; and (3) assessing patient and family health outcomes and satisfaction. Allow the co-location strategy to achieve its maximum level of implementation (at least one year) before making a final assessment of its value and sustainability. D. Develop mechanisms for obtaining input from pregnant and postpartum members who screen positive for maternal depression on alternative service options that meet their needs and preferences.
Behavioral health practices and providers in the HealthChoices network	Explore opportunities to co-locate behavioral health specialists at nearby physical health practices that currently do not have in-house behavioral health capacity. Develop a detailed plan for (1) integrating the individual or function into the practice's clinical work flow and providing access to relevant information systems; (2) fully utilizing motivational interview techniques and patient-centered principles; and (3) assessing patient and family health and satisfaction. Allow the co-location strategy to achieve its maximum level of implementation (at least one year) before making a final assessment of its value and sustainability.

Table S.6
Recommendations to Improve Overall Systems Performance in Relation to Maternal Depression Screening, Referral, and Engagement in Treatment

Stakeholder	Recommendation
Pennsylvania Department of Public Welfare, Office of Mental Health and Substance Abuse Services	Effective screening, referral, and treatment engagement enhances the quality of life and functioning of women with maternal depression and reduces a risk factor that can negatively affect a young child's development. These outcomes support the department's goals of enhancing the development of young children and increasing opportunities for persons dependent on Medicaid to obtain employment. In this context, it is critical to establish maternal depression as a priority in the public mental health system.
Pennsylvania Department of Public Welfare, Office of Medical Assistance Programs and Office of Mental Health and Substance Abuse Services	A. Accelerate collaborative interdepartmental efforts to encourage the development and proliferation of interoperable electronic health records for improving data sharing and integration and coordination of care throughout the commonwealth. B. Enlist MCOs in a coordinated effort to develop common standards, metrics, and incentives for enhancing network providers' use of health information technology options that support integrated care. C. Charge the physical and behavioral health care coordination groups within each HealthChoices zone to develop collaborative strategies for (1) increasing rates of maternal depression screening and (2) improving referral and treatment engagement rates of pregnant and postpartum members who screen positive for maternal depression.
HealthChoices physical and behavioral health MCOs	A. Work together with providers, consumers, and families to develop information-sharing agreements as needed for ensuring full knowledge of issues that affect a woman's physical and behavioral health or the health of the mother and the child. Specific efforts should be made to develop a standard release-of-information form for use by MCOs and network providers serving similar patient populations. B. Create regular opportunities (e.g., in-person workgroups, teleconferences, webinars) for care managers and physical and behavioral health providers to review shared cases of success and failure related to serving pregnant and postpartum women who screen positive for maternal depression.
Physical and behavioral health practices and providers in the HealthChoices network	A. Identify appropriate health information technology options that support integrated care and funding opportunities or reduced cost programs for developing them. B. Continue to track progress on screening, referral, and engagement in treatment for women at high risk for maternal depression and develop and implement internal quality-improvement programs as needed. C. Advance efforts to network with other area providers who are treating pregnant and postpartum women who screen positive for maternal depression to share resources, experiences, and learning.

because of developmental concerns related to medical or environmental risks (e.g., very low birth weight, elevated blood lead levels). Third, it seeks to address primary-caregiver depression and the related challenges of healthy early childhood development through home-based, family-centered interventions designed to strengthen parenting and the parent-child relationship.

The Allegheny County Maternal and Child Health Care Collaborative has made a long-term commitment to building a model system of care for parents and young children in the community. While we at the collaborative have made significant progress during the past eight years, there is still much work to be done. We hope that the report will inspire others to mobilize forces in their communities and beyond to strengthen the systems responsible for ensuring the health and well-being of all families across the commonwealth.

> Depression is real after childbirth—for both mothers and fathers. It is the people who touch the lives of new parents that can make a difference in a family's life. It is the people that we trust that can make us feel safe enough to talk about the unhappy feelings that sometimes occur after a new baby comes into our life. . . . This project can make a difference . . . for the health of our future—our families.
> —*mother, Allegheny County, Pennsylvania*

Organizations and Leaders Participating in the Allegheny County Maternal Depression Initiative

Physical Health Practices and Providers

Children's Hospital Primary Care Center
Debra Bogen
Evelyn Reis
Marnie Weston*

Magee Women's Hospital
Andrea Aber
Peggy Brady
Diane Dado*
Pamela Dodge*
Christine Eisom
Veta Farmer
Lisa Karow
Candace Manspeaker*
Terri McKenzie
Connie Nelson
John Silipigni
Cynthia Slosar*
Nina Sowiski*
Margaret Watt-Morse*
Christina Weiss

UPMC Family Medicine Practices
Terri Rosen
Jeannette South-Paul

UPMC Family Medicine–McKeesport
Tracey Conti
Shari Holland
Jeanne Puskaric
Nina Tomaino*

UPMC Family Medicine–Saint Margaret's
Jonathan Han
Linda Mischen
Sukanya Srinivasan
Melissa Williams

UPMC Family Medicine–Shadyside
Seth Rubin*
Lisa Schlar
Lisa Treganowan
Ann O'Donnell

West Penn Allegheny Health System
Linda Chrillo*
Marian Jonnet
Laurel Milberg
Katherine Neely
Rowena Pingul-Ravano

Behavioral Health Practices and Providers

Mercy Behavioral Health
Carol Frazer
Paula Scandrol

Milestone
Kieran Giovannelli
Ken Wood

Mon Yough Community Services
Noreen Fredrick
Gina Gargarella
Carol Lingsch
Leanna Plonka

TCV MH/MR
Gail Kubrin
Louise Meleshenko
Josie Ulrich

Western Psychiatric Institute and Clinic
Jack Cahalane
Jewel Denne
Frank Ghinassi
Roger Haskett
Carolyn Hughes
Kelly O'Toole
Katherine Wisner

Westmoreland County MH/MR
Sara Gumola

Local Medicaid Managed Care Organizations

Community Care Behavioral Health
Susan Carney
Mary Doyle
James Gavin
Julie Hoyt
Kristen Johnson
John Lovelace
Kimberly Riley
James Schuster
Sherry Shaffer
Carole Taylor
Deborah Wasilchak

Gateway Health Plan
Michael Blackwood
Patricia Boody
Pedro Cardona*
Michael Coughlin*
Leslie Hawthorne
Stacey Hudak
Vicki Huffman
Mona Jordan Hawkins
Renee Miskimmin
Maria Moutinho
Patricia Soltan
Chris Ann Uhler

Unison Health Plan
Demetrois Marousis
Diane Reilly
Joseph Sheridan
Peggy Tate
Sheila Ward

UPMC *for You*

Kim Fedor
Wendy Hoffman Raviotta
John Lovelace
Debra Smyers

Value Behavioral Health

Laverne Cichon
Mark Fuller
Mary Johnston
Cynthia Kemerer
Karyl Merchant
Angie Sarneso

Local and State Payers and Policymakers

Allegheny County Department of Human Services, Office of Behavioral Health

Marc Cherna
Regina Janov
Patricia Valentine
Karen Webb
Gwen White

Allegheny County Health Department, Maternal and Child Health Programs

Bruce Dixon
James Gloster
Pamela Long
Roberta Patrizio

Pennsylvania Department of Health

Melita Jordan

Pennsylvania Department of Public Welfare

Jane Boyer
Mary Diamond
Joanne Grossi
Cecilia Johnson*
David Kelley
Barbara Molnar
Estelle Richman*
Linda Zelch

Community Organizations

Birth Circle

Irene Frederick
Cynthia Salter

Early Head Start (COTRAIC)

Deborah Gallagher

Early Head Start (University of Pittsburgh)

Vivian Herman

Every Child, Inc.

Susan Davis*
Dennis Falo
Sean Meredith

Family Resources

Charma Dudley
Andi Fischhoff
Marcia Warren

Healthy Start

Cheryl Squire Flint
Joanne White

Local Foundations and Other Supporters

Eden Hall Foundation
Sylvia Fields
Jordana Stephens

FISA Foundation
Dee Delaney*
Kristy Trautmann*

Highmark Foundation
Yvonne Cook
Christina Wilds

Staunton Farm Foundation
Joni Schwager

UPMC Health Plan
Diane Holder
Kevin Kearns*
John Lovelace

RAND–University of Pittsburgh Health Institute

Jacob Dembosky
Ray Firth
Sarah Frith*
Donna Keyser
Sandraluz Lara-Cinisomo*
Susan Lovejoy
Sajith Pillai*
Harold Alan Pincus
Dana Schultz
Gina Snyder
Shannah Tharp-Taylor

* Organizational affiliation and/or position has changed since the start of the initiative. List compiled June 1, 2010.